ON THE BRINK

The Petrodollar Crisis…
and how it will affect YOU

BERNICE JENSEN

Printed in the United States of America.

ISBN 978-1-300-75947-8

TABLE OF CONTENTS

INTRODUCTION

The war that's begun, and the war to come

There is a war brewing around the world – a secret war, one you haven't heard of unless you've been listening very closely, but a real war nonetheless – and one that can change your life for the worse.

It's coming. And all we can do it prepare for it.

In this book, I will do my best to explain the coming conflict, and give some suggestions on how you can best weather the coming storm. I'm not an economics expert or a survivalist; I'm just someone who cares about my own future, and the future of my family and friends. I want, really, what we all want: to be safe and secure; to leave the people I love a world that is better than the one I inherited myself …

… But the coming petrodollar war threatens all of that. It's time for us to become aware of it, and to prepare for the coming disaster.

It's not the best news you've ever heard. But it may be some of the most important.

Read on …

THE BASICS

First, it's important to understand some of the basic terminology and economic realities of the world around us. Let's begin with that.

What is a "petrodollar"?

We all know what a "dollar" is. It has been the single most powerful unit of value in this country and throughout the world for more than a century – the greatest century of economic and technological development in human history.

But do you know what a "petrodollar" is?

It is a unit of exchange, just like the bills in your wallet, but its role in the world economy and your future is almost entirely different than the "dollar" you have known and trusted for your entire life.

A 'petrodollar' is a United States dollar earned by a country through the sale of petroleum to another country.

The term originated with economist Ibrahim Oweiss of Georgetown University almost 40 years ago, in 1973. He recognized even then that the "petrodollar" had an entirely different role in international finance than the dollar in general – that the world needed a term that could describe the dollar *specifically* received by the members of the Organization of the Petroleum-Exporting Countries (OPEC) in exchange for oil. (You'll also hear the term "oil currency" in the books and speeches relating to the petrodollar; it means essentially the same thing.)

Petrodollars serve an entirely different purpose than domestic currency – the dollars that you and I use to buy food, secure shelter, and acquire some level of comfort and security. Petrodollars are really a measure of wealth on an international level – the unit that countries use to measure how much they have earned (or spent) on the single most vital substance in the modern world: not gold, not food, not water ... but *oil*.

The behavior, effects, *importance* of the petrodollar is distinctly different than the domestic dollar … and its future are intimately linked to your own.

Because it's a near certainty that a war is coming – a *petrodollar* war – that will affect you, your family, and your standard of living.

What is "petrodollar warfare"?

The term itself was coined by William R. Clark, who wrote a book by that title. It refers in general terms to the global conflict – thus far, largely economic – that is currently simmering between nations, both developed and developing. It is the struggle to control the vital and dwindling finite resource we call oil; ultimately, it is the struggle to manipulate and control the world's economy, often at the expense of countries other than your own (and maybe – only *maybe* – your allies).

Petrodollar war transcends ideologies. It is a faceless, apolitical movement. And it is approaching a crisis level that will dwarf the military conflicts of the past, from our own Civil War to the World Wars to the Cold War.

What makes the petrodollar so important?

Most oil sales throughout the world are denominated in United States dollars (also known as "USD"). And most countries rely on the import of oil to keep their economies running (including, ironically, countries with the capacity to drill and refine oil on their own; it is an international webwork that penetrates both oil *importers* and oil *exporters.*) Because of this reliance, these countries must maintain large stockpiles of dollars, called *reserve currency,* so they can continue to buy and import oil throughout any fluctuations in local or national economic stability. It is an issue of *savings,* not *cash flow.* And at the moment, those savings are almost entirely U.S. Dollars.

What is "reserve currency"?

A **reserve currency**, or **anchor currency**, is a currency that is held in significant quantities by many governments and institutions as part of their foreign exchange reserves. It also tends to be the international pricing currency for products traded on a global market, and commodities such as oil and gold.

Holding these foreign, internationally traded currencies in bulk allows the issuing country to purchase the commodities at a marginally lower rate than other nations, which must exchange their currencies with each purchase and pay a transaction cost. For major currencies, this transaction cost is negligible with respect to the price of the commodity. It also permits the government issuing the currency to borrow money at a better rate, as there will always be a larger market for that currency than others.

How does being a "reserve currency" affect the dollar at home?

The international demand of U.S. dollars puts an upward pressure on the dollar, regardless of the 'real' economic issues of the United States at any given moment. In fact, this continuing demand gives the U.S. government far more flexibility in handling, saving, spending, and printing money that it would if it had to rely *only* on domestic conditions.

The huge international demand for U.S. dollars as *petrodollars* allows the US government to gain revenues through *seignorage*, a complex economic shell-game that allows the U.S. government to make money simply through the process of moving that money around … and by issuing bonds at lower interest rates than they otherwise would be able to. This means higher budget deficits at a more sustainable level than most other countries can enjoy. It also means that the price of oil is more stable in the U.S. than anywhere else, since importers do not need to worry about exchange rate fluctuations.

BRUTAL ECONOMICS 101

This "flexibility" – what some would call "lack of discipline" – regarding the money supply gives the U.S. Government and its agencies a great many more options when it comes to managing economic problems and even crises.

Generally speaking, the government has only four alternatives to exert economic influence:

1. Increase income by **raising taxes**
2. Reducing costs by **cutting spending**
3. **Borrowing money** by issuing government bonds
4. **Printing money**

Raising taxes and making meaningful spending cuts are both terribly unpopular, even in times of hardship or crisis. Borrowing money is less noticed, but it has its own limitations. But *printing* money is essentially invisible to the general public: they simply don't notice it, and it has no immediate affect – no burden on the individual, no loss of services.

Printing money does, however, have one huge drawback: *inflation*. If a country prints more and more money to pay for goods and services primarily within its own borders, the price of those items will increase to absorb those new dollars, and in the modern world it can happen very quickly, and fly out of control even more quickly.

But robust international trade can forestall that inflation. The newly printed dollars can 'fly' overseas in the form of petrodollars, hiding the immediate domestic effect, sometimes for years, and giving the government in questions a nearly inexhaustible ability to borrow and spend, spend and borrow.

Welcome to the United States of America in the 21st century.

Check your money: What is a "Federal Reserve Note"?

Have you ever asked yourself why the U.S. Dollar is called a Federal Reserve Note? That is because the dollar is issued by the Federal Reserve and then *loaned* to the United States government. And because our dollars are loaned to our government by the Federal Reserve, which is a private central banking cartel, *the dollars must be paid back ... with interest.*

Who sets the interest rate on the loaned dollars? The Federal Reserve, of course, just like the bank that lends you money to buy a car or a house sets its own interest rates on that loan.

Obviously, then, the Federal Reserve has a clear vested interest in maintaining a stable and growing global demand for U.S. dollars: it wants it loans repaid, with interest. And like any business venture fighting for its life, it will do *anything* to ensure the survival and success of its clients – particularly its largest client, the United States of America.

The threat and the opportunity: the U.S.A.'s addiction to oil

We've heard about this for all of our adult lives, so frequently it has lost much of its impact and meaning. But this old cliché is actually very important to our future survival as a nation: *The United States economic is absolutely reliant on foreign oil,* and there is no sign that we are systematically ending, or even reducing, the level of addiction.

If the flow of oil from beyond our shores was cut off tomorrow, the U.S. economy (and thus the world economy) would collapse in a matter of days or weeks. There simply isn't enough petroleum and petroleum products produced domestically, or enough in our "strategic oil reserves" – to allow the U.S. to function for any significant period of time.

Here is the key concept:

U.S. markets are addicted to oil and its derivative products (jet fuel, diesel fuel, gasoline, etc.) for their energy needs.

Therefore, the price of oil can be an important political factor, and our country's energy policies, foreign policy, and economic well-being are dependent on the price of oil *and* the abundance and easy movement of the petrodollar. Bottom line: the United States is *absolutely dependent* on the continued use of the U.S. Dollar as the primary, if not exclusive, unit of exchange for oil.

… and conversely, political enemies and economic rivals of the United States are *very* interested in seeing oil denominated in some other currency: euros, pounds, yen, or yuan.

INTERNATIONAL CURRENCIES: A HISTORICAL REALITY

Since the invention of nations, and since trade between those nations became a reality, the world has needed to measure commerce between those countries – they have always needed an *international currency,* and almost always the fortunes of one particular nation over all others has benefited from the use of their domestic coin as the unit of international exchange.

As economist Avinash Persaud says, "International currencies in the past have included the Chinese *liang* and Greek *drachma*, coined in the fifth century B.C., the silver *punch-makred coins* of fourth century India, the Roman *denari*, the Byzantine *solidus* and Islamic *dinar* of the middle-ages, the Venetian *ducato* of the Renaissance, the seventeenth century *guilder* and of course, more recently, sterling and the dollar."

For the first half of the twentieth century, the most popular interntional currency was the *pound sterling*, and the United Kingdom benefitted hugely from its dominance in international trade.

But after the Second World War, things changed. The international financial system was governed by a formal agreement, the Bretton Woods System (see below). Under this system the United States dollar was made the centerpiece of international commerce; the U.S. government even guaranteed the central banks of other nations that they could sell their U.S. dollar reserves for gold at a fixed rate. Because of this change, European countries and Japan devalued their currencies against the dollar so they could increase exports and bolster their developing or recovering economies. It was that international dollar that empowered the rebuliding of the world after 1945, and the system worked to almost everyone's advantage for almost twenty years.

Then problems began.

THE FUTURE OF INTERNATIONAL CURRENCY

Will this always be the case? Will one country's currency always dominate international commerce, or will some other unit of exchange, one unconnected to any specific sovereignty be created? Economists disagree. Some believe that a single reserve currency will always dominate the global economy. The argument is that, in the absence of sufficiently large shocks, a currency that dominates the marketplace will not lose much ground to challengers.

Other economists disagree, especially when it comes to the denomination of official reserves. As long as the currency's market is sufficiently liquid, they say, the benefits of *diversification* are strong. Diversification ensures against large capital losses.

These economists believe that the world may soon begin to move away from a financial system dominated uniquely by the U.S. dollar. There was actually some movement in that direction a hundred years ago, before the World Wars, when multiple currencies shared the status as primary reserve currencies. True, the British Sterling was the largest currency, but the French franc and the German mark shared large portions of that market ... until they were all replaced by the U.S. dollar.

How is the top reserve currency selected?

The top reserve currency is generally selected by the banking community for the strength and stability of the economy in which it is used. Thus, as a currency becomes less stable, or its economy becomes less dominant, bankers may over time abandon it for a currency issued by a larger or more stable economy.

This can take a relatively long time. It is not an official or even particularly logical process. For example, it took many years after the United States overtook the United Kingdom as the world's largest economy before the dollar overtook Sterling as the dominant global reserve currency. And this is precisely why the *perception* of stability or dominance plays such an important part in petrodollar politics ... and petrodollar warfare.

A TOUR OF THE WORLD'S RESERVE CURRENCIES

Though the U.S. dollar dominates, in fact most countries keep a wide range of currencies in reserve for international trade ...

The U.S. dollar

As of 2013, the U.S. dollar is the most widely held reserve currency in the world. Throughout the last decade, an average of two thirds of the total allocated foreign exchange reserves of countries have been in US dollars. This makes it easier for the United States to run higher trade deficits, and in many ways allows it to blunt inflationary effects from "too much money" in a sluggish economcy, and to postpone any domestic currency crisis.

The dollars reserves held by central banks, however, is tiny in comparison to the reserves held by private holdings. And therein lies the problem:

If the major holders of reserve currencies –
petrodolalrs – decide for any reason to shift those
holdings into other currencies, the consequences for
the U.S. economy could be devastating.

The Euro

The euro is currently the second most commonly held
reserve currency, comprising approximately a quarter of
allocated holdings. This strength is a direct result of the
previous strength of the German deutsche mark, the
second most important currency reserve after that
country's defeat in the Second World War.

When the euro was launched in 1999, it replaced the
mark, the French franc, and ten other European
currencies, and inherited the status of a major reserve
currency. Since then, its contribution to official reserves
has risen continually as banks seek to diversify their
reserves and trade in the euro zone continues to expand.

In 2007, former U.S. Federal Reserve Chairman Alan Greenspan said the euro could replace the U.S. dollar as the world's primary reserve currency. It is "absolutely conceivable that the euro will replace the U.S. dollar as reserve currency, or will be traded as an equally important reserve currency."

He is not alone in this assessment. Econometric analysts Jeffery Frankel and Menzie Chinn suggested in 2006 that the euro may replace the U.S. dollar as the major reserve currency as early as 2020 ... if the member of the EU, including the UK and Denmark, adopt the euro by 2020, and/or if the recent depreciation of the dollar persists continues.

In recent years, the euro's share of the worldwide currency reserve has continued to increase—albeit at a slower rate than prior to the worldwide credit crunch.

The Pound Sterling

The United Kingdom's pound sterling was the primary reserve currency of much of the world in the ninteenth century. The emergence of the United States as an economic superpower (and, just as important, the establishment of the U.S. Federal Reserve System in 1913), along with U.S. economic dominance from the second half of the 20th century onward and economic weakness in the UK at various intervals during the second half of the 20th century, resulted in sterling losing its status as the world's most reserved currency.

Beginning in 2006, the pound began to re-establish itself. Analysts say this resurgence is caused by investors considering the pound as a stable high-yield proxy to the euro, as well as the position of London in world financial affairs.

The Japanese Yen

Japan's yen is part of the International Monetary Fund's (IMF) "special drawing rights" (SDR) valuation. The SDR currency value is determined daily by the IMF, based on the exchange rates of the currencies making up the basket, as quoted at noon at the London market. The valuation basket is reviewed and adjusted every five years.

The SDR Values and yen conversion for government procurement are used by the Japan External Trade Organization, for Japan's official procurement in international trade. It is this relationship that has restricted the otherwise powerful yen (powerful, at least, at certain times over the last one hundred years) as a major player in currency reserve … thus far.

The Swiss Franc

The Swiss franc is often considered a reserve currency, because of the perceived stability of the currency and the Swiss banking system. However, the share of all foreign exchange reserves held in Swiss francs has historically been well below 0.5%. The daily trading market turnover of the franc however, ranked fifth, or about 3.4%, among all currencies in 2007.

The Canadian Dollar

A number of central banks (and commercial banks) keep Canadian dollars as a reserve currency. In the economy of the Americas, the Canadian dollar plays a similar role to that played by the Australian dollar (AUD) in the Asia-Pacific region. The Canadian dollar (as a regional reserve currency for banking) has been an important part of the British, French and Dutch Caribbean states' economies and finance systems since the 1950s. The Canadian dollar is also held by many central banks in Central America and South America.

Canadian economists primarily define and value the Canadian dollar in terms of the United States dollar; economists can therefore indirectly observe internal behaviours and patterns in the U.S. economy indirectly, by observing how the Canadian dollar floats in terms of the U.S. dollar. Though it is now considered a petrodollar, the Canadian dollar only fully evolved into a global reserve currency in the 1970s when it was floated against all other world currencies. Some economists have attributed the rise of importance of the Canadian dollar to the long-term effects of the elimination of the gold standard that effectively ended the Bretton Woods system of global finance. In 2007 it was ranked 6th in value held as reserves.

The Chinese Yuan

The Chinese yuan or renminbi (RMB) cannot be used as a reserve currency as long as the Chinese government maintains capital controls on the conversion of its currency. Holding the currency would not be attractive to central banks unless China develops a strong open bond market. Because of this restriction, less than 0.9% of all currency market transactions were carried out in renminbi, as of 2010.

Chinese President Hu Jintao has said that it would be a long process before the yuan will be accepted as a global currency. However China has taken modest steps in this direction with currency-swap agreements with a few western Pacific nations.

CALL FOR NEW MAJOR RESERVE CURRENCY

In the last few years, there has been a rising chorus of calls to abandon the U.S. dollar as the single major reserve currency. The United Nation Conference on Trade and Development demanded such a change as recently as 2010, in a report that pointed out the dangers of basing reserves on a single currency, or even multiple national currencies. Instead, they urged the creation of a more stable global financial system. Just a few months earlier, in 2009, then-President of Russia Medvedev proposed a new 'world currency' as an alternative reserve currency to replace the dollar.

Chinese representatives have been quoted as saying, "we don't want to make any more foreign exchange reserve of any paper currency, because all the paper currencies are government debt currencies."

China, Russia, India, Turkey, Brazil, Venezuela and oil-producing countries have recently agreed "to transact all of their mutual trade and investment in their own currencies," effectively minimizing the need, at least in the short term, for a global reserve currency.

And yet oil is still priced in dollars, which has brought complaints about OPEC's policies of managing oil quotas to maintain dollar price stability.

The effects of this mounting trend are just beginning to be felt.

THE 1944 BRETTON WOODS CONFERENCE

In the final days of World War Two, an economic conference in Bretton Woods, New Hampshire effectively changed the world for decades to come.

The conference took its name from the small town where it was held. There, 44 leaders from all of the Allied nations met to create a new global economic order – one that would be dominated by the victor in the long conflict, the United States of America.

In addition to introducing a number of global financial agencies, the historic meeting also created an international gold-backed monetary standard which relied heavily upon the U.S. dollar.

Initially, this dollar system worked well. However, by the 1960's, the weight of the system upon the United States became unbearable.

Today, the "Bretton Woods System" that prevailed for the next twenty-five years or more is looked upon as a time of unprecedented stability and growth on the international stage. But it all began to change in 1971, with what has often been referred to as "the Nixon shock" – the removal of the U.S. dollar from the gold standard.

1971: THE END OF THE INTERNATIONAL GOLD STANDARD

After more than two decades of stability, the Bretton Woods system of reliance on the U.S. dollar as the unit of international exchange began to show its age. By the late 1960's, deficit spending in Washington was uncontrollable, as the expenses of international conflict and domestic social programs strained the government's resources.

At the same time, the global economy had become dependent upon a sound U.S. economy. Japan, Germany, France, the UK – all still recovering from the devastation of World War Two even twenty years later, were still largely dependent upon a financially stable American economy. But as the decade ended, U.S. trade deficits had reached unsustainable heights, and the perception of the United States' impeccable economic stability was being challenged around the globe.

Behind it all, informed economists were deeply concerned about another more complex and less obvious problem: the growing imbalance of U.S. gold reserves to debt levels.

Because of the wars and social programs, the United States had acquired massive new debt but did not have the money to pay for them. At the same time, U.S. gold reserves were at all-time lows, exacerbated by the growing demand of other countries requesting gold in exchange for their dollar holdings – an arrangement made at Bretton Woods decades earlier.

The original purpose of the Bretton Woods system is not to make the Unite States the gold repository for the global economy. It was in fact, meant to generate worldwide trust in U.S. paper money, simply by knowing that those notorious reserve notes *could* be converted into gold at any time. And that trust system had worked extremely well for a lifetime …

… but no longer.

In the early 70s, European and Asian countries began to doubt America's ability to manage their own finances … and began to 'cash out' by converting larger and large portion of their reserves into gold.

The Nixon Administration was faced with two alternatives: massively reduce spending, increase taxation, and reduce its existing debt … or increase the dollar price of gold to accurately reflect the new economic realities. But neither alternative was attractive politically or socially.

President Nixon chose a third alternative. In August of 1971, he announced that U.S. dollars would no longer be redeemable in gold, effective immediately. It was a decision that became known to economists as the "Nixon shock," and its effects were immediate and felt around the world.

The "Nixon shock" and the supply of money

By removing the link between gold reserves and the U.S. Dollar post-1971, the U.S. government effectively gave itself the ability to value its own currency – what is known in economic circles as a *fiat* currency that is worth what it is worth in goods and services only because the government issuing it says so. Economists also refer to it as a "floating" currency – one that does not derive its value from anything external, and when the dollar became a "floating" currency, the rest of the world's currencies, which had been previously fixed to the dollar, suddenly became "floating" currencies as well.

The Nixon Administration's decision did something more. It allowed the government to print money at will, and to take the pressure off the country's gold reserves.

But the immediate and major concern was the role of the U.S. dollar in foreign exchange. Now that it was no longer backed by gold, would foreign nationals still use it as the overwhelmingly preferred reserve currency? And further, what would restrain the U.S. from spending whatever amounts it liked, and simply funding it by printing more money, empowering a potentially apocalyptic inflationary spiral.

Clearly, some other economic buffer was needed to retain trust in the U.S. dollar and shore up governmental spending habits, in the face of foreign wars and exploding domestic programs.

Enter the petrodollar.

THE PETRODOLLAR SYSTEM

The "Nixon shock" that untethered the U.S. Dollar from the gold reserve came about in the summer of 1971. Less than two years later, Saudi Arabia and the United States created a whole new standard, when Saudi Arabia agreed that *every barrel of oil purchased from the Saudis would be denominated in U.S. dollars.*

Under this new arrangement, any country that sought to purchase oil from Saudi Arabia would be required to first exchange their own national currency for U.S. dollars. In exchange for Saudi Arabia's willingness to denominate their oil sales exclusively in U.S. dollars, the United States offered weapons and protection of their oil fields from neighboring nations, including Israel.

Quite logically, of course, this would lead to a major change in U.S. foreign policy. If the health of the dollar on the international stage was linked inexorably to petroleum, then it was obviously in the best interests of the United States to protect and preserve those countries that, by dint of geology and luck, produced the vast majority of the oil they needed so badly. Those countries included:

- Bahrain
- Egypt
- Iraq
- Israel
- Jordan
- Kuwait
- Oman
- Qatar
- Saudi Arabia
- United Arab Emirates
- Yemen

By 1975, all of the OPEC nations had agreed to price their own oil supplies exclusively in U.S. dollars in exchange for weapons and military protection, thereby creating the entity known as *the petrodollar*.

According to the agreement, the United States would offer military protection for Saudi Arabia's oil fields, including weapons and other armament and – implicitly or explicitly – protection from Israel. In return, the Saudis agreed to transact their petro-business in dollars only, and to invest those profits heavily in U.S. debt securities.

By 1974, the petrodollar system was firmly in place. By 1975, all of the oil-producing nations of OPEC had fallen in line with nearly identical arrangements. To all intents and purposes, the gold standard had been replaced by the petrodollar system, and the U.S. was free to continue its debt-ridden fiscal policies … at least for a while.

Today, virtually all global oil transactions are settled in U.S. dollars. And if a county does not have a sufficient reserve of U.S. dollars, they need to obtain them, through the foreign exchange markets or export deals with the U.S. Take Japan as an example. With very few natural resources and a large demand for oil, Japan creates its dollar surplus for oil through a massive export plan. Think of the automotive industry alone (i.e., Honda, Toyota, Subaru).

But the robust petrodollar system had its limits. True, the system created an immediate and largely artificial demand for U.S. dollars around the world, and that demand grew as the demand for oil itself grew. At one level it allowed the United States to continue to grow and develop for years based on its *fiat* currency … but at the same time it made the U.S. domestic economy extraordinarily vulnerable.

Since the dollars are no longer backed by hard assets, they rely entirely on *belief* … and on their continued heavy use. So if enough countries *stop* believing in the dollar and stop using it in vast quantities … everything changes for the worse.

In recent years, several countries have veered from the petrodollar system. Iran, Syria, Venezuela, and North Korea are among those countries, while China, Russia, India and others are choosing to use their own currencies for oil, rejecting the notion of international currency reserves to begin with.

The consequences of this gradual but very real abandonment can be severe.

U.S. Foreign Policy: An Oil-Based Agenda

U.S. foregin policy – and what some would call adventurism, or even imperialism – was focused primarily on Indochina during the 1950s, 60s, and 70s. Many assumed that the shift of attention from that region in the 1980s had to do both with the defeat of the U.S. in Viet Nam and the weakening and collapse of the Soviet Union and therefore its own plans for economic domination.

But the shift from the gold standard to the petrodollar has had as much to do with U.S. foregin policy, and war itself, as the geopolitics of Europe – perhaps more. Because key to the agreements made, first with Saudia Arabia and soon thereafter with the rest of the OPEC nations, called for serious, significant and long-term *military* commitment to stability in the Middle East…even at huge costs to the American people and the U.S.' long-term allies around the world.

The balancing act that is the Middle East

On the one hand, the U.S. has been, and remains (at least publicly) a staunch ally of Israel. On the other hand, the U.S. is also committed, not so publicly, to the protection and stability of the OPEC nations, despite those countries' domestic policies, hatred of Israel, and public anti-U.S. pronouncements. The result is a convoluted and often dangerous foreign policy that has resulted in three wars, a series of covert "support" operations, and the birth of a new militarist Israel in response to the growing lack of faith in American commitment.

When you are considering America's place in the Middle East, consider these facts:

- Israel's sworn enemies receive eight times more in foreign aid than Israel does.

- As early as 1973 – within months of the agreement with Saudi Arabia, President Richard Nixon said, that military intervention to protect U.S. strategic oil supplies in the region "was a strong possibility."

- In 1980, the U.S. created the RDJTF, the Rapid Deployment Joint Task Force, with the stated mission of maintaining regional stability and the flow of oil through the gulf.

- In 1983, then President Jimmy Carter transformed the RDJTF into UCENTCOM, the United States Central Command, responsible for the Middle East and Central Asian regions. This year marks the thirtieth anniversary of that mysterious and powerful force.

Target: Iraq

We could spend many pages – in fact, a whole different book – on the sequence of events that led to and from 9/11 and the second war in Iraq. What seems very clear, more than a decade after it began, is that there is *no* credible evidence linking the attack on the World Trade Center to the government of Iraq or leader Saddam

Hussein … and that the Bush Administration had plans, even prior to 9/11, to mount an assault on Iraq with the intent of creating a politically stable, obedient, and permanent "home base" where U.S. and international oil interests could operate without difficulty. Here are just a few facts:

- One year before 9/11, the U.S. began constructing a billion-dollar military base in Qatar called "Al Adid," whose sole purpose was to serve as a staging area for U.S. military actions.

- Bush's former counter-terrorism director, Richard A. Clarke, has said, "The president in a very intimidating way left us, me and my staff, with the clear indication that he wanted us to come back with the word there was an Iraqi hand behind 9/11 because they had been planning to do something about Iraq from before the time they came into office. I think they had a plan from day one they wanted to do something about Iraq. While the World Trade Center was still smoldering, while they were still digging bodies out, people in the White House were thinking: 'Ah! This gives us the opportunity we have been looking for to go after Iraq."

- On October 7, 2001, Operation Enduring Freedom was launched. Thousands of U.S. troops were sent into the mountainous regions of Afghanistan ... but the Administrations focus was always on Iraq.

- Again, Clark has said that the war was not based on, "violence or terrorism, but something very different, yet not altogether surprising – declining economic power and depleting hydrocarbons." In fact, he claims that on September 24, 2000, Saddam Hussein "proclaimed that Iraq would soon transition its oil export transactions to the euro currency." By 2002, Saddam had fully converted to a petroeuro.

- Iraq's oil supplies are estimated to be among the largest in the world.

It is, of course, impossible to prove exactly what U.S. intentions were in the Iraq war – a conflict that ultimately ended doing more harm than good, both to regional stability and the U.S. economy, And Bush himself publicly denies that oil was the motivation. "The idea that the United States covets Iraqi oil fields is a wrong impression," he said. "I have a deep desire for peace. That's what I have a desire for. And freedom for the Iraqi people". Colin Powell as well said, "This is not about oil; this is about a tyrant, a dictator, who is developing weapons of mass destruction to use against the Arab populations." Secretary of Defense Rumsfeld and virtually every key member of the military-industrial complex denied that it was "about oil." But the 'real' reason for the Iraq War was never clear. Weapons of mass destruction? A link to 9/11? Terrorist camps?

Denials aside, there were occasional moments of plain-spokenness. Paul Wolfowitz, for instance, one of the architects of neoconservatism and a close advisor to George W. Bush, said in 2003, "Let's look at it simply. The most important difference between North Korea and Iraq is that economically, we just had no choice in Iraq. The country swims on a sea of oil."

Even former Chairman of the Federal Reserve Alan Greenspan, in his book *The Age of Turbulence,* says, "I am saddened that it is politically inconvenient to acknowledge what everyone knows: the Iraq war is largely about oil."

Target: Afghanistan

Even before – and even after – the wasteful and destabilizing war in Iraq, there was Afghanistan. The invasion began in October of 2000, weeks after 9/11, with "Operation Enduring Freedom." The official reason was to liberate Afghanisan from Al Qaeda," and secondarily to find and capture or kill Osama bin Laden. The first goal was never quite achieved, though it changed shape and structure repeatedly in more than ten years of conflict. The second was only accomplished long after George W. Bush left office.

The war in Afghanistan has become America's longest running war. Twenty thousand Afghans and more than 2,000 Americans have lost their lives there, tens of thousands more have been injured and disabled. And even now, as the last of the official troops are returning home, it is not clear how many U.S. troops will remain in Afghanistan after 2014 to provide "counterterrorism and training support." Certainly the largest conflicts are over ... but our commitment to Afghanistan has not ended.

How did we get into this position? What possible value could this rocky, arid land have?

To put it simply, Afghanistan and all of Central Asia is one of the world's last untapped treasure trove of petroleum and strategic minerals. It has been estimated that the entire Caspian Sea is full of oil and natural gas , starting from Azerbaijan and continuing to the opposite shore in the territory of Kazakhstan and Turkmenistan. These energy deposits take on enormous importance given their close proximity to the rising energy hungry powers of China and India. The dwindling oil production from Alaska and the North Sea makes these untapped resources even more valuable. To further sweeten the pot, it was reported in 2010 that the Pentagon and American geologists had discovered vast amounts of untapped mineral deposits in Afghanistan worth nearly $3 trillion. (In fact, the existence of the deposits of these valuable strategic minerals has been known for a long time; these 'announcement' gave more details, but only made a long-time private discussion far more public.)

For decades, Central Asia has held immense strategic geopolitical significance. During World War II, for example, Adolf Hitler enacted Operation Blue in an attempt to capture the Caucasian oil fields from the Russians. His hope was that this victory would help him secure his plot for global domination. His failure left the oil-rich region of Central Asia under Russia's control.

In fact, throughout history, countries have attempted to invade and exploit Afghanistan and all of Central Asia's abundant natural resources…and each of them have had to deal with the harsh reality of one major obstruction: the region is isolated and landlocked. And to one devastating degree or another, each of the empires of the past crashed and died in Afghanistan's rocky mountains.

Today, Western powers are once again racing to build an empire in Central Asia. But, unlike the last century, this New Great Game is not about controlling the lands of Central Asia. Instead, as Karl Meyer and Shareen Brysac put it in their book, Tournament of Shadows: The Great Game and the Race for Empire in Central Asia , "pipelines, tanker routes, petroleum consortiums, and contracts are the prizes of the new Great Game".

Target: Iran

Now, of course, there is question of Iran. With Iraq fading into memory and Afghanistan winding down, Iran is being touted as the next major theater of conflict for the Middle East. At base, the Iran is being characterized as a nuclear threat, with evil intentions of building nuclear weapons. In fact, the 'difficulty' with Iran is far more complex than that, and – not suprisingly – based on oil and energy.

For many years, Iran has pursued the idea of building a pipeline that would deliver natural gas – which the country has in abundance – to Pakistan. The project was first proposed by a Pakistani civil engineer named Malik Aftab Ahmed Khan in the 1950s, and Iran and Pakistan began formal discussions about the project as early as 1994. Over time, the plan expanded: Iran sought to extend the pipeline through Pakistan and into India.

The U.S. did not approve of the project; it would likely interfere with pipeline plans of their own. The U.S. began to put pressure on India and Pakistan; ultimately, they backed out of the arrangement in 2009, shortly after signing a civilian nuclear deal with the United States. More recently, U.S. Secretary of State Hillary Clinton has threatened Pakistan with sanctions if the country continues with the pipeline plans. Currently, the agreement calls for both Iran and Pakistan to construct their own pipelines by the end of 2014. Iran has already completed its section of the pipeline; Pakistan has turned to Russia for additional funding. And now, despite attempts to inteview or even bribe Pakistan, the Iran-Pakistan pipeline project is slated to begin operations in December 2014 as scheduled.

Meanwhile, the debate in the U.S. about Iran as a nuclear threat has reached new heights ... despite the fact that Iran has no known nuclear devices, that Iran has not invaded its neighbors in decades, Iran denies wanting a nuclear bomb.

Is the growing pressure to "do something about" Iran due, if only in part, to its plans to destabilize the oil supply structure of the Middle East? And where will this pressure lead us in the current and future administrations? Only time will tell, but one thing is cerain: *oil,* and its free and unfettered flow to the West, will continue to be a major factor in Middle East policy...and in the conflicts to come.

THE COMING COLLAPSE

It was said at the beginning of this book, and it bears repeating: the world is addicted to oil. And for all the talk about alternative energy and renewable resources, the world will continue to be addicted to oil and all its derivatives for the forseeable future.

Currently, the people on planet Earth consume nearly 90 million barrels of oil per day. According to some projections, global oil demand will reach well over 100 million barrels per day by 2015. And as the global demand for oil increases, the petrodollar system guarantees that the demand for the U.S. dollar increases with it. This artificial demand for U.S. dollars has provided remarkable benefits for the U.S. economy. America's standard of living has never been higher.

This decades-long 'boom' – despite downturns and recessions – can only continue as long as the demand for the US. Dollar and U.S. debt securities remain strong. The petrodollar system shores up America's economy; it has for decades.

THE CONSEQUENCES OF PETRODOLLAR COLLAPSE

Just how serious is this? After all, the United States survived the Great Depression of the 1930's, two World Wars, a see-sawing economy for decades after and even the Wall Street and real estate meltdowns of 2008. How does the potential, perhaps inevitable, collapse of the petrodollar measure up to the other economic upheavals of the last 100 years?

To paraphrase a popular movie of the past, if you rated all the financial disasters of the past on a scale of 1 to 10, the collapse of the petrodollar would be an 11. Or worse.

Here are just a few of the major upheavals you could expect if the system collapsed:

- Foreign nations would begin sending a flood of U.S. dollars back to the United States, in an effort to convert them (through whatever means) into whatever new currency required to purchase oil

- As a result, the Federal Reserve would be far less inclined to print more money to cover current debt, since it could no longer be 'hidden' in overseas reserves

- That, in turn, would result in an immediate and catastrophic increase in interest rates – rates that have been hovering at historical lows since 2008

- Hyperinflation would be a likely result, at least until new interest rates took hold

- The housing market, only beginning to recover as of 2013, would almost certainly collapse yet again, as low-interest loans became impossible to secure and the pool of borrowers for high-interest loans shrank

- Business loans and credit would become scarce, even non-existent

- The price of gas and other oil-based products (fuel oil, kerosene, even plastics) would skyrocket

- Washington would almost certainly reduce the amount of money in the system in an attempt to slow the hyperinflation, leading to an even higher increase in interest rates

- Businesses and individuals with adjustable-rate loans or credit balances would find their existing debts would be suddenly unmanageable. Layoffs and business closures would be inevitable.

- The prices of assets – homes, businesses, income properties – would crash

… And that is only the beginning.

So has the process already begun? Economic movements move with glacial speed, but there are already signs that the petrodollar system is in jeopardy.

THE RETREAT FROM THE DOLLAR

As we have discussed, the U.S. dollar has functioned as a *de facto* 'world currency' for more than a generation. As of 2010, U.S. dollars made up more than 60 percent of all foreign currency reserves in the world.

But things have begun to change. The previously unshakeable confidence in the strength of the dollar has been shaken repeatedly, especially since the banking scandals and economic collapse of 2008. Today, a series of international agreements are in place or being developed and have made the U.S. dollar less important in international trade. This could be setting the stage for a fundamental shift in the way that trade is conducted around the globe…and if the petrodollar dies, the U.S. economy will be in serious, serious trouble virtually overnight.

Here are eleven recent developments that seriously jeopardize the future of the petrodollar system:

- China and Russia have begun to use their own currencies when trading with each other.

- Brazil conducts more trade with China than any other country Already the largest economy in South America, a recent "currency swap" deal between China and Brazil is an attempt to safeguard both parties from serious losses should any global financial crisis ensue.

- China and Australia also recently agreed to a huge currency swap deal with China. In fact, China is structuring similar deals with many countries – Australia and Brazil are just the largest in an expanding group – that ultimately will promotes the international use of the yuan, making it a possible challenger to the U.S. Dollar as the international currency of choice. Other similar deals are in place with South Korea, Turkey and Kazakhstan.

- China And Japan are entering into a series of agreements that will promote direct trading of the yen and yuan without using dollars, encouraging the development of a market for companies involved in the exchanges. Japan will also begin to buy Chinese bonds. China is Japan's biggest trading partner with 26.5 trillion yen ($340 billion) in two-way transactions in 2010.

- India and Japan have also agreed to a large currency swap deal, a major rescue for the rupee, India's unit of exchange, which is widely considered the worst-performing currency in Asia.

- Iran is still selling oil; they simply don't do it using U.S. dollars. China and India, their biggest customers, are trading oil for food and consumer products. India is using its own currency, the rupee, to pay a large portion of its bill thorugh its central bank. And oil-for-wheat deals are in the works (and perhaps already in place) with Pakistan, Russia, and perhaps other countries. There are all schemes whose primary purpose is to circumvent the UN-imposed sanctions, but they all contribute to the overall sense that there are other ways to buy and sell oil, beyond the previous unassailable U.S. dollar.

- Iran and Russia are using their own currencies in a bilateral trade agreement.

- China and Chile are in the midst of a major expansion of trade between the two nations, and is also likely to lead to significant currency swaps.

- China is actively looking to enhance cooperation in mining, expand farm product trade, and promote cooperation in farm product production, processing and agricultural technology, as well as participate in infrastructure construction and transportation development.

- China and the United Arab Emirates have recently agreed to a very large currency swap deal, to "boost trade and investments" between the two countries.

- China and Africa trade exceeds $100 billion, making China, Africa's largest trading partner.

Each one of these agreements is an increasingly ominous indication of the weakening grip of the U.S dollar on international commerce. The largest countries in the world – whole continents – are finding new mechanisms to exchange wealth, new ways to purchase oil and other resources that circumvent or even replace the petrodollar and U.S. currency as the de facto "global" currency. What was essentially unthinkable even a decade ago is now entirely 'thinkable,' and countries around the world know it. And no country is more aware of the changing world than China …

CHANGING THE EQUATION: CHINA AS OIL MAGNATE

As we can see from the series of currency swaps and bilateral trade agreements, China is already well aware of the vulnerability of the petrodollar system, and more than willing to take advantage of its growing weakness.

China is also willing and capable of altering the *supply* side of the oil equation as well. With billions of development dollars at its disposal, and with billions of barrels of crude under their territory and control, China is making a separate and equally serious set of moves to become a significant refiner and supplier of oil in all its forms – and global entity to rival the megacorporations, individual countries, and even OPEC.

Recently, Saudi Arabia and China – already the second largest consumer of oil in the world – have teamed up to begin work on a massive new oil refinery to be built in the Red Sea port city of Yanbu. China already imports more oil from Saudi Arabia than the United States does, and at this moment they still make all those purchases in U.S. dollars. But will the use of the petrodollar continue if China and Saudi Arabia are business partners?

This $8.5 billion joint venture, scheduled to open in 2014, will cover an area of about 5.2 million square meters and process 400,000 barrels of heavy crude oil per day. Aramco, Saudi Arabia's national oil agency will retain 62.5% ownership, with the balance going to China's wholly owned company, Sinopec.

At the same time, China is making deals with several other important oil producing nations.

- China is underwriting the building of the largest oil refinery every in Egypt.

- China has signed a $23 billion agreement to construct three gasoline refineries and a fuel complex in Nigeria.

Keep an eye on the international financial news: this is clearly just the beginning of a continuing trend: a China strategy to interpenetrate the global "oil engine" at every level: as consumer, refiner, shipper, and supplier. And nothing could be a greater threat to the current petrodollar system than Chinese manipulation.

WHAT TO WATCH FOR

At this moment, the petrodollar system still reigns supreme, and the U.S. dollar dominates as the *de facto* "world currency." That strength, however fragile it might be, continues to allow the United State to pay debts and incur new ones based on the vast reserves of U.S. locked up overseas by virtually every developed nation in the world.

But the cracks are beginning to appear. Change *is* coming, and though it may be slow in its approach, when it finally comes – like the "Nixon shock" of 1971 – the results could cascade as swiftly and do as much damage as the three-day Wall Street collapse of 2008 …and worse.

Here are just a few of the things to watch for:

Watch Saudi Arabia

Saudi Arabia remains the largest supplier of petroleum in the Middle East, and in many ways the most politically stable political entity in the region. If and when Saudi Arabia announces a move away from the petrodollar system, that will be a major trigger event for the global financial system.

Watch Iran

Like Iraq and Afghanistan before it, Iran is the current and future focal point for conflict. The mainstream media will continue to follow Washington's lead and characterize Iran as a nuclear threat, while ignoring its geopolitical role in the continuing and escalating resource war.

The question is will the powers in control really risk World War III by attacking Iran, a key ally to Russia and China? After all, it may still be sometime before Iran would be able to develop even a single nuclear weapon, not to mention a delivery system that could reach significantly beyond its own borders; it has no military capability to target the U.S. and it has not attacked another country since 1978. Still, with economic sanctions and a massive propaganda machine already at work, the clock is ticking.

Watch China and Russia

Every developed country in the world is keeping large reserves of U.S. dollars to pay for oil, and the U.S. has benefited from that process for almost half a century. But the currency reserves of two countries in particular dwarf the reserves of all other countries combined: China and Russia.

They warrant close observation. Though it's unlikely they will simply and brutally decouple themselves from the petrodollar system in a single stroke, they have already begun to experiment with other ways to sidestep the petrodollar through bilateral trade agreements, cash swaps, and co-ventures. Look for more of this in the future…and for *modifications,* rather than complete abandonment, of the petrodollar system in favor of the euro or the yuan – the two most likely candidates.

Watch the Federal Reserve

Obviously, those who have the power to print the dollar out of thin air have the most to lose if the dollar was to fall. Since 1913, that power has been held by the Federal Reserve. And it is more than worth noting that the Federal Reserve is a *private* entity, owned by a conglomerate of the most powerful banks in the world. The Reserve is not constrained by law except in the most general sense; it has an entirely separate and often obscured agenda beyond the most simplistic: survival as the single most powerful entity in international commerce. How far are they willing to go? How much are they willing to lose to maintain that position?

Much of what the Reserve does is shrouded in secrecy, but there are a growing number of journalists and analysts watching their every move. Pay attention; though the Reserve's activities are often obscure, they are always meaningful, and can provide insight into the current situation and future developments.

Obviously, the creation of the petrodollar system was a brilliant political and economic move. Washington was acutely aware in the early 1970's that the demand curve for oil would increase dramatically with time. Therefore, they positioned the dollar as the primary medium of exchange for all global oil transactions through the petrodollar system. This single political move created a growing international demand for both the U.S. dollar and U.S. debt — all at the expense of oil-producing nations.

HOW TO PREPARE

The future is never certain. Though the facts point to an end to the petrodollar system sooner rather than later, and to a financial upheaval unlike any we've ever seen, nothing is absolute.

Still, it makes sense for you to prepare yourself and your loved ones for the worst: a swift and unexpected (by most) economic adjustment that could change the world virtually overnight.

There are many books on preparedness and survival that are worth reading. Most of them agree on these basic points:

Stock up. It's unrealistic to think that any family or even neighborhood could survive independent of the outside world for an indefinite period, but it is entirely reasonable to stock up on essentials, from food to purification equipment to medications and toilet paper (don't forget the toilet paper) that could sustain your family for two to four weeks without aid. The cost to go much beyond that level is prohibitive for almost everyone, but being prepared for an extended period of isolation can be comforting. Let's just hope it's never needed.

Educate yourself. A mainstream medium—which includes television news funded by international conglomerates for *either* side of the ideological fence – are ultimately answerable to their bosses, not to 'us.' The information they supply is, almost by definition, slanted towards one direction or another, and built on an often unspoken agenda. Fortunately, the internet, independent publishing, podcasts and blogrolls can offer the careful researcher a number of alternatives.

Learn about the petrodollar crisis and the related issues of international politics, multinational corporations (particularly the energy, manufacturing, and agricultural sectors), and the new breakthroughs in energy and materials science that could change our world overnight. It requires extraordinary vigilance, judgment, and commitment ... but you can't anticipate the future if you don't understand the present.

Convert a portion of your assets into "permanent" wealth. There are few items that seem to retain value, but there is no harm and much good in converting a *portion* of your personal wealth from Federal Reserve paper to some other form – a form that will retain its value despite changes in monetary policy or inflation. Gold, of course, is the easy and most common example. Blue jeans or even uncut denim or other durable cloth is another. Most foods are too perishable for long-term storage, but some resist aging, including chocolate in its most basic form, salt, and some canned goods. Water purification technology and tablets; hand-cranked radios and lighting systems, tools for construction – all of these have a value that is common, and are often not considering in doomsday' scenarios. It would be foolish and unnecessary to clean out your bank accounts entirely and switch to "survivalist" mode; on the other hand, enriching yourself and your family with objects of usefulness, beauty, and permanent value can make you more comfortable and serve as a possible hedge against future instability.

Remain watchful. You've already begun by purchasing this book. Now do more: keep an eye out. Learn what sources of information you can trust. Read and listen carefully. You'll be obligated to put it all together *yourself*, because few in the media will do it for you, and most who do have hidden agendas of their own.

Even though economic policy may move slowly, the world itself moves fast. It took decades for the fiscal crisis of 2008 to build up to a critical point; it took only hours for the world to lose a third of its paper value, and just a few days longer for the world to change. And look at how quickly foreign policy changes – the Patriot Act, Guantanamo, the wars in Iraq and Afghanistan – were instituted after that horrible day in September 11.

It can happen all too quickly. We must keep watch.

Have hope. It's a big world, with more than six billion people interacting in a nearly infinite number of ways. It is, in fact, a *chaotic state,* and though this may be a terrifying concept at one level, it is oddly comforting at another: *good* things can happen as often and as unexpectedly as *bad.*

There are also a great many good people with your best interests at heart are still working ever day in the banking industry, the government, the media, and technology. They have saved us and raised us up many times – quite literally more times than we know – and they will do it again.

We just need to learn and watch, be prepared and be ready … and have hope.